PREFACE

This publication has been produced in response to requests by visitors during tours of the caves as a guide for an account of what may be seen in the caves. It is also an attempt to chronicle their history and, since the origins of the caves are somewhat obscure, a reflection on some of the popular theories pertaining to them.

I would like to record my thanks to fellow members of the Local History Group for their assistance whilst compiling this booklet, and acknowledge the assistance provided by the Dorking and District Museum, whose library is the source or verification of much of the contents.

My thanks also to Messrs. H.Pearman and J.Henderson of the Chelsea Speleological Society for permission to reproduce their plans of the caves, and to Miss Mary N. Felgate for allowing me to reproduce the extract from "A Dorking Childhood - Memories of Old Dorking."

Finally, I would like to thank my wife, Shirley, for all the typing and other assistance given towards producing this booklet.

Cliff Weight

South Street 1871     Courtesy of MVDC     Plan of caves

The plain wooden door set into the wall beside the War Memorial in South Street gives no indication to the casual passer-by that it provides access to a unique part of Dorking's past. Behind this self-effacing door is the town's only remaining complex of caves accessible to the general public, albeit by prior arrangement.

**********************

Dorking has long been known for the number and extent of its caves and passageways, particularly in the town centre. None of these is believed to have been natural - the easily worked nature of the greensand of this area apparently encouraged digging and the results were durable. Thus there were many such excavations to be found, especially along the High Street and South Street. Alas most have now been filled in or bricked up; those still remaining are generally privately-owned and used as cellars or for storage.

The South Street caves were also originally privately owned, part of the old properties which once fronted the road and which were demolished almost 70 years ago. Until then that part of the road between Butter Hill and Junction Road had a very different appearance to the present day scene.

Indeed, until the last century, part of the market was held in South Street. Dorking being a thriving market town, the farmers came to sell their livestock in the main market area of the cobbled East Street (now High Street). Their wives set up stalls in South Street to sell their butter, cheese, eggs and other produce. Possibly this is the derivation of the name Butter Hill, which still survives today as the short stretch of road leading from South Street to Victoria

Demolition, South Street 1919

Courtesy of Dorking & District Museum

Terrace; some say, however, it is a corruption of 'Borough Hill'. South Street was also the site of the annual fair prior to its removal to Cotmandene. Polling booths were erected in the street for elections, and men gathered here for enlisting in the First World War.

As a result of the increase in traffic which followed the arrival of motor vehicle, it was decided to widen the road. The block of premises fronting South Street between Butter Hill and a point opposite Junction Road was demolished in 1919. Sadly the old cottages, shops, post office and police station were no more. Although over the years they had deteriorated through neglect, they had presented a picturesque scene similar to those in the present day West Street. In fact, the pictures of them are often mistaken for views of West Street, which fortunately survives and is now a part of the Conservation Area.

The demolition of these buildings was followed by the erection of a bandstand (removed in 1963 and replaced by the existing flower tubs and seats) and the War Memorial. One can imagine, therefore, that with the road only half its present width, the entrance to the caves before 1919 was even more obscure since it was tucked away behind one of the old cottages.

*********************

There have been only a few literary comments on the caves, notably:-

The historian John Aubrey (1626-1697) who wrote

> In this Town is a great Plenty of Cherries, particularly a wild Cherry that Mr. John Evelyn

> tells me makes a most excellent Wine, little inferior to the best French claret, and keeps longer; and no where are finer Caves for the Preservation of their Liquor than in the Sand here.

John Timbs (in his "Picturesque Promenade Round Dorking," published in 1822) said:-

> Dorking being situate on a sandy rock, abounds with deep and capacious caves or cellars which are extremely cold, even in the height of summer. The most remarkable of these is one on the left side of Butter Hill, which runs for a considerable distance in an angular direction. On the side of the entrance, is a wide staircase curiously cut out of the rock and descending by fifty steps to a crystalline spring of water, which is forty feet perpendicular beneath the entrance cave. About a century ago, an individual expended the whole of his property in digging this cave and, having thus wasted several hundreds, he is said to have died in the poor house. The cave is now more profitably used by a respectable distiller of the town as a wine cellar, an appropriation differing widely from the original design of its projector.

> The house, under which this artificial excavation partly extends, was upwards of sixteen years the residence of the Rev. John Mason, chiefly known for his work entitled "Self-Knowledge."

John Dennis (in his "Handbook of Dorking," published in 1858) also mentions them:-

The large cellars or caves beneath the town, dug out of the sand rock, are highly curious. It is said that more than a hundred years ago a man was foolish enough to expend all his property in making the largest of these excavations, at the bottom of which there is now a spring of pure water.

The minimum height of the passages is six feet and the maximum 11 feet (on the stairs); the minimum width is just under four feet and the maximum just over eight feet (in the first cellar). Why they were dug as high as 11 feet is not known since six feet is adequate for the majority of people nowadays, let alone years past when the population tended to be shorter. However, bearing in mind the unusual height and width of the excavations and the extent of the caves, it can be imagined that a very large tonnage of sand was removed. Indeed between the first and second flights of stairs, on the two turns, there are grooves cut into the walls which are suggested as being the marks made by ropes used to haul sacks of sand up to street level.

Once on the surface, where was the sand put? It may have been scattered around or used as infill. One theory is that so much sand was required for the rebuilding of the City of London after the Great Fire of 1666 that it was all carted there; it has even been said this need was the reason for the excavations in the first place. As 1672 is the oldest date found inscribed in the caves so far, it does tie up rather nicely with that idea but it is not really practical since there was plenty of sand readily available on the surface, not just in Dorking but throughout the length of the greensand valley, stretching as it does for several miles to the east and west of the town.

Of other theories for the excavation the most credible is that recorded by Timbs and Dennis, that it was a gentleman's folly, the small circular cavern 50 feet beneath the street level being the centre piece, dating from the late 17th Century; it is in this cavern and the lower part of the stairs which give access to it, that most of the older dates are to be found. The story of the wealthy gentleman having spent all his money to pay for the digging of the folly has a certain irony of fate. If he did end up in the poor house he was then able to view the results of his expenditure from close quarters since the poor house in those days was only a short distance away on the opposite side of the street, a little way beyond the junction with Vincent Road.

There is a carved bench all the way round the cavern suggesting that even if it was not the initial owner's purpose, later occupiers used it as a meeting place or a 'haven from the outside world'. One suggestion is that it was hiding-hole during periods of religious persecution and it could even be this was the reason for the existence of the cavern. The date of 1672 is in the well shaft but another which could be 1666 (although dubious) is by the lower part of the stairs. Certainly there was in the 1660s persecution of the Puritans who did not accept the 1662 Act of Uniformity which prescribed the form of public prayers, administration of the sacraments, and other rites in the Church of England. This was followed by the Conventicle Act passed in 1664 which censured meetings of dissenters to the established Church. The following year the Five Mile Act forbade any minister who had refused to sign the Act of Uniformity to teach and live within five miles of any town. There is evidence of a passageway just inside the caves entrance leading to another cave still in existence beneath a nearby residence. Although the house was rebuilt circa 1725 with later additions, there is a shaft leading to the attic from that cave which has no obvious purpose. The Declaration of Indulgence in 1672 by Charles II suspending penal laws against Recusants was withdrawn the next year: it was not until 1688 that a fresh Declaration passed by James II exonerated Non-Conformists.

Another persecution of the 17th Century was that of 'The Fifth Monarchy Men'. These were members of a fanatical sect who proclaimed about 1645 that the Millenium was at hand, when Christ would return to earth and establish the Fifth Universal Monarchy (after those of Assyria, Persia, Greece and Rome). They declared themselves 'subjects of King Jesus' and said no government ought to rule mankind until His coming. Cromwell dispersed them in 1653 but eight years later the sect revived and became 'a menace to the public peace', incurring their repression and causing them to go to ground. Perhaps this is literally what they did in Dorking, where it is known a group of members was active and it could be that they became the occupiers of the cavern.

From the plan on page 19 it can be seen that the lower flight of stairs passed close to the main well shaft but the upper flight actually cuts through part of the shaft, implying that the well was excavated before the stairs and cavern. The depth of water at the foot of this well remained at approximately four and a half feet for many years causing a black stain to form round the walls. There were many springs in the neighbourhood and the water here emanated from one or more of those springs following a course towards the lowest point of the town, viz The Pippbrook, and on to the River Mole.

This gives rise to a further legend that there was at one time a boat or raft hidden at the bottom of the well. This is referred to in the reminiscenses of Dorothy Ellen Tyson (nee Langdon) who was born in 1885. These were edited and published in 1979 by her niece as 'A Dorking Childhood - Memories of Old Dorking'.

The visitors who came to number 19 from time to time were proudly taken round Dorking's famous Beauty Spots ... and even the intriguing narrow little alleyways between the older houses of the Dorking streets were of much interest - but for the Langdon's visitors the most thrilling was the Cave.

This alleged Smuggler's 'back entry' cave was then in possession of Tom Langdon's Employer, who used the upper part of the cave as his Wine Cellar, and Tom was in charge of the key. The cave, which ran right back into the ground under Victoria Terrace, had its unassuming entrance, between two small cottages in South Street. Looking like an old barn door, nobody's interest was attracted, and most people concluded it was a sort of back gate entrance for the cottages. What the cottagers themselves thought about the mysterious doorway between them is not known. Perhaps they did not even realise it was there and none seemed curious enough to try to break the lock on the old door.

Visitors arrived and the 'Creaking' old door was duly opened and shut again ... and in single file, between rows of cobwebby bottles (port here was over 40 years old) and queer little kegs on

South Street looking north-east c. 1910

Courtesy of Dorking & District Museum

the dry earth floor, the little procession wended its way. Every other one carried a dripping candle (battery torches were not invented) and after the bottle racks had been passed, one came to a narrowing passageway that ended in earth steps that wound round and round into blackness below. The air was good, however, for several airshafts (presumed to come up in the gardens of the Victoria Terrace houses), gave a glimmer of light as well. After descending three or four 'flights' of well graded steps cut into the sandstone, one approached the Mystery ... for at one's feet gleamed a River ... black and silent and not a little terrifying. Here the underground stream was about 18 feet wide, and most mysterious and thrilling of all against the opposite wall, and well out of reach in the deep water laid the wreck of an old boat.

Rumour said that this stream connected up with the River Mole, over a mile away, and was used by the occupants of Betchworth Castle (now an old ruin) either as an 'escape' or more likely for smuggling purposes. In an attempt to confirm this, two lads obtained a light canoe, and were alleged to have got permission to explore the stream. They found the 'ceiling' had fallen in further down, although the stream still continued to flow as usual. The wreck was certainly of a fair sized rowing boat, suitable for small cargo, and how it got there was a mystery for it was quite impossible to have been carted down those winding steps, so this seems to prove that the underground river has some outlet. The River Mole too disappears into the ground near

Betchworth Castle (hence its name) but History has never recorded the truth, and quite likely some nefarious trade forbade publicity.

The notion of the stream connecting to Betchworth Castle does seem rather fanciful, as does the size of the boat. Perhaps in the eyes of a child a spring becomes a stream and a small craft becomes a boat. Certainly the idea of smuggling and the presence of a small vessel have some slight credence since an 18th century Act forbade the keeping of boats within three miles of an inland waterway without a licence. This was an anti-smuggling measure and in consequence many boats were concealed.

Also in earlier days the water level in Dorking, as elsewhere, would have been much higher. As a result of the increase in the town's population, which was particularly notable during the 19th century, the amount of water used greatly increased. Towards the end of that century and in the early part of this century, with the population still growing, the improvement in pumping methods, and the increasing availability of mains water the level was even further reduced. Nevertheless, according to a reported incident, there was still sufficient water in the South Street Well for an official of the Council on a visit in 1920 to get quite wet when he accidentally fell in! It is estimated that nowadays the water level in this particular area is a further 50 feet below the base of the well so there is no chance of a further ducking.

The more recent excavations in the caves are the two wine cellars and their two connecting passageways on the top level, presumably dug less than 200 years ago as the oldest date appears to be 1815. The atmosphere within the caves complex affords ideal conditions for the storing of wines and spirits, since it is virtually dry (just a small amount of condensation) and with a constant temperature throughout the year of approximately 50 degrees Fahrenheit, fluctuating by only one or two degrees.  This is particularly noticeable on visits to the caves on hot summer days, when inside it is pleasantly cool and on cold winter days when it is cosy and warm inside.  Following upon the ownership by the original person or persons responsible for their being dug the caves remained in private hands until early this century.  Various local brewers and wine merchants, of which Dorking for a small town seemed to have more than its fair share, became owners and users of the cellars, notably members of the Cheesman and Young families.

Of the several liquors stored here, one was cherry wine; the town was noted for the abundance of cherries, as mentioned by John Aubrey.  At some stage walls four feet high and three feet wide were erected in the two cellars in order to divide the bottles of liquor into manageable categories.  A wooden racking system was used to stock the bottles in these divisions, or bins as they were called.  Each bin could hold upwards of 700 bottles and since there were 40 bins, the capacity of the cellars was up to 28,000 bottles!  In addition to this the remainder of the complex, i.e. the connecting passageways and the cavern, had space for more bottles or other provisions as required.

Little wonder then that these caves, as indeed many others in the town, had a reputation for being smugglers' haunts.  According to J. S. Bright in his "History of Dorking" published in 1884 the practice of smuggling was very prevalent in the Holmwood, and there was, from the South Coast to London, an established method of communication, with depots at convenient distances. This illegal traffic was maintained by the connivance and co-operation of the villagers and others on the road. There was, at that time, a prevalent laxity of feeling upon the subject of smuggling, while occasional large profits, and the pleasure of drinking spirits so cheaply, attracted many to share in the undertaking. This practice has been discontinued through the greater vigilance of the Coast Guard, the change in duties upon many articles, and probably to the increase of temperance in the population generally.

Although there is no firm evidence that they were so used, the South Street caves with their several well-concealed entrances would have afforded an ideal place to store contraband. This is particularly true of the upper level where, if necessary, the smugglers could make a quick getaway, but would they have occupied the cavern at the bottom where, if caught, there would be no escape? - we can only guess. However it is almost certain that no initials would have been carved in the walls by these clandestine characters as they were not in the habit of leaving records of their existence!

The wine merchants and brewers remained owners of the caves until 1912 when the executors of Youngs sold them to the Dorking Urban District Council. The storage of spirits continued as the Council leased the Caves to wine merchants, the last to make use of them being H. G. Kingham & Company, who had a wholesale business in Station Road, together with several retail premises. Their main shop was originally situated on the south side of the High Street but later moved to Clock House which was on the opposite side of the road (where Seeboard now have their showrooms). Kinghams also used the caves to store various other provisions which benefited from the equable temperature.

H.G. Kingham & Company vacated the caves during the 1960s and it was in 1970 the Dorking and Leith Hill District Preservation Society took over the lease. The Society's purpose was not only to ensure their preservation but also to make the caves accessible to the general public by means of conducted tours. The management of the latter was vested in the Historical Group (now The Local History Group) a branch of the Society which, since its formation in 1967, had shown a few parties round by private arrangement. The conducted tours continued until September 1975, when, due to the tramp of many pairs of feet, the steps became so badly eroded they were considered to be unsafe to the public. The Council had new steps cut and concreted but to only half the width of the original ones in order that the original work could still be seen; also a handrail was installed as a further safety measure. The work having been completed, the caves were re-opened in June 1977, and have remained so since. To date the number of visitors since 1970 is over 6,000.

It has been questioned whether Dorking Caves were used as air-raid shelters during World War II but there is no record of the South Street caves being used for this purpose. However one or two caves behind the shops on the south side of the High Street were prepared for such use with extra ventilation installed, and others were probably used on an unofficial basis.

From their inception the caves would have been lit by candles or rush light or by lanterns of some kind. During tours they are still lit by candles (augmented by guides' torches). These candles apart from being more practical than electricity, give a feeling of affinity with bygone days. Considering there is now only one entrance, it is surprising that there is quite a marked circulation of air. This is particularly noticeable on the stairs, where the candles not only flicker but burn down and need replenishing quite frequently.

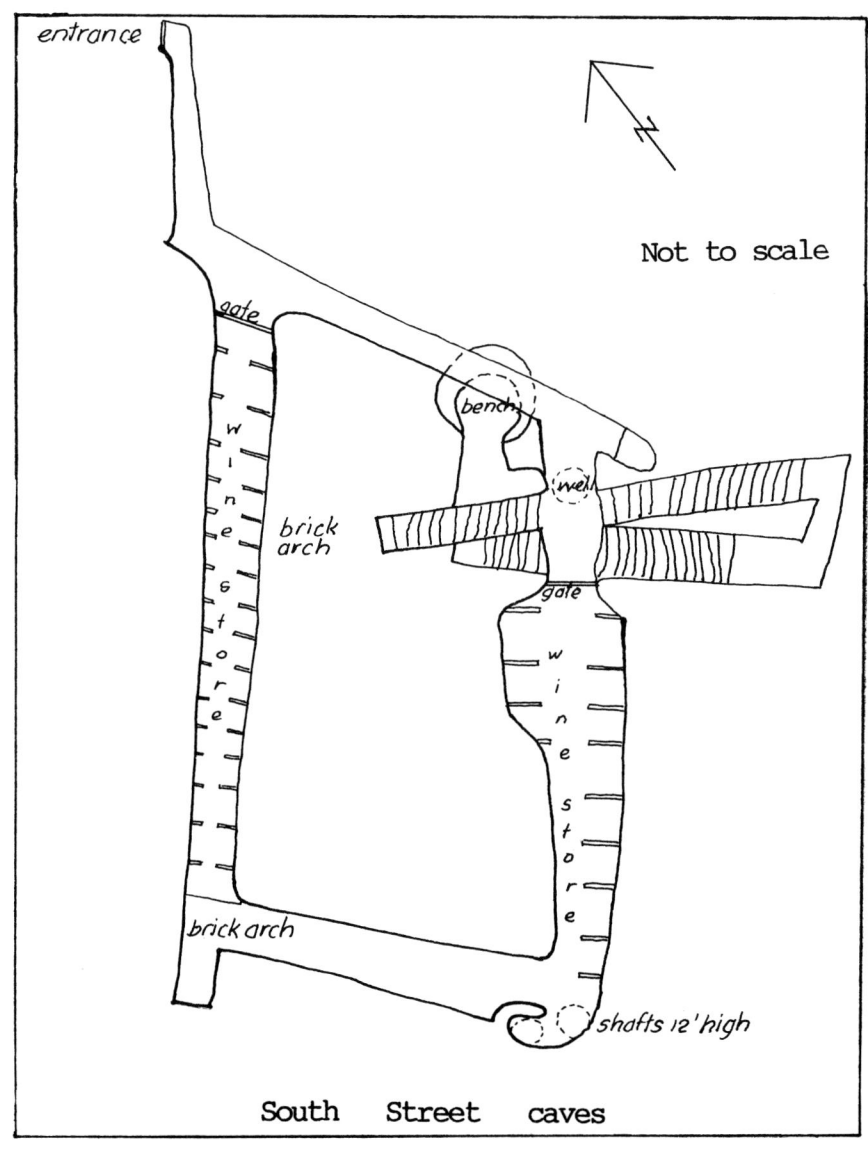

Plan by kind permission of J. Henderson and H. Pearman

## TOUR OF THE CAVES

Upon entering the Caves, immediately to the left is a bricked-up entrance to a passageway believed to have led to a cave further down South Street under a private residence. Turning sharp right there is a slight downward incline where, at approximately 15 feet distance, is a bricked-up arch on the right, the earlier entrance to the Caves prior to the erection of the War Memorial. The passageway now takes a right-angled turn away from that arch and, at a few feet on the right-hand side is the entrance to the first of the two wine cellars. Before entering this cellar, there is to be seen in a niche to the right, the first example of inscribed lettering and dates. This is carved 'AUST 1890' or 'AUGT 1890', suggesting August of that year.

In the cellar, which extends about 60 feet and is over eight feet wide, are wine bins lettered A to F on the left and returning G to K on the right. When F is reached, there is a step down and the bins continue but now numbered instead of lettered, 1 to 9 on the left and returning 10 to 18 on the right. At bin No. 1 is the initial WC and the dates 1815 and 1818; at bin No. 2 is carved the name Cheesman (John Cheesman was the registered occupier in the late 18th century). At bins 4, 9 and 18 are tally marks, presumably of the number of bottles withdrawn from store, though what unit each mark denoted is not known. The initials WK and the date 1836 appear in two bins, Nos. 9 and 11; bin 12 has the date 1832 and the initial GCK.

Above bins 12 and 13 is a band of the ironstone indigenous to the sandstone of this area. At bin 17 are the initials FDV and PF, but no date. It is said that the black deposit which appears on the walls and covers most of the roof takes at least 40 years to accumulate and therefore most of the dates and initials seen are considered genuine. An example of a faked date may be seen at bin No. 3 where someone has been tempted to inscribe the date 1735. Not only does the fact that there is no black deposit on it indicate it is hoax, but from research, it is believed that this cellar would not have been in existence until well after that date! At the end of this cellar a brick wall was erected some time ago, making it impossible to continue in that direction, necessitating the retracing of steps to the cellar entrance, at which point on the opposite wall may be seen the more recent initials of GER and EC.

Turning right, a five feet wide passage leads for 52 feet away from the street. There are no carvings of any significance here but it does give rise to an enigma. Looking back towards South Street entrance, it can be seen that the roof is well over six feet high except for the left hand side where a recess extending the length of the passage is much lower. Two theories have evolved so far, one that the lower height was originally uniform across the width of the passage and over the years as people grew taller or tired of banging their heads, the roof was made higher but not for its full width. The other, more credible, theory is that having hauled sacks of sand up from the depths to ground level, a donkey was led to and fro with the sacks as panniers on his back, making transportation of the sand so much easier. Certainly the height of the recess lends itself to this theory. However, this is conjecture and a true answer may yet be established.

The end of the passageway is situated underneath the rear of the houses of Victoria Terrace. Large steps lead upward and advance the passage even more to what was another exit at some stage, possibly in the garden of one of the old cottages which were situated on the high ground before they were replaced by the Victorian buildings. Why the steps were so big is a mystery although, since they formed two ledges, they could have been used to stand on when passing goods up to or down from the exit.

Turning right again, the main well shaft is the next item of interest. In order to cross it, the floor has been brick-arched then covered by a metal plate. The shaft is not quite uniform in diameter, being 48 inches wide in one direction (across the passage) and 52 inches in the other direction. This is wider than the other two shafts further on and much wider than normal well dimensions, suggesting that this may have been used by the cottagers on a community basis. The bricked-up top of the well, ten feet above, emerges about three feet above the ground in the private garden belonging to one of the houses in Victoria Terrace; from that point the well extends to a depth of 75 feet. In the passageway and set slightly into the wall on either side is a recess up to six feet high presumably where a gate was situated, perhaps as a later security measure to bar access from the well to the cellars, or to the stairs, as the cellars themselves had gates at their entrances. Inscriptions on the wall here are CI, EF, IC, and CM.

After the well shaft, and beyond the flight of stairs, is the second cellar with the wording above the entrance 'Vintage Ports'. This cellar is 44 feet long and seven feet wide except for the first 13 feet where a recess has been cut either side to make an almost circular chamber 14 feet at its widest point. Both sides of this chamber have a ledge cut, presumably for use as a seat. There are three bins each side of this chamber, nos. 19-21 on the right, and nos. 22 to 24 on the left; at bin no. 23 is the name ROPKE (or KOPKE) and the date 1917. After the chamber the bins continue on the left hand side only, nos. 25 to 29. At bin no. 25 is the name TAYLOR, 26 is DELAFORCE 1912, and at 29 SANDEMANS 1912.

Adjacent to bin no. 29 is the second well shaft

and, six feet away, as the passageway takes another 90 degrees turn to the right, is the third well shaft; both are just over 36 inches in diameter. They were filled in with sand to the floor several years ago, although re-excavated in 1984 to a depth of about four feet below the floor level. During this excavation work, a few pieces of pottery and bits of animal bones were unearthed but sadly nothing of value or interest. However, who knows what may have been buried further down? For safety reasons no further digging has been made to date, but with suitable anchorage and equipment further work may well be undertaken in the future. Small niches have been cut on opposite sides of both shafts, either to accommodate a crude scaffolding arrangement or for use as hand and foot holds to enable a person to brace himself against the wall to ascend or descend. The top of the shafts, 19 feet above, are bricked over in the same way as the main shaft.

The passage extends 45 feet back towards South Street, and is mainly eight feet wide. Unlike the other passageways, this one has been dug unevenly, particularly the roof, which is very roughly hewn and only just six feet high at its start. Possibly this was a later addition to the original excavations, and used purely as a connecting passageway. In fact, at its end, through a hole in the brickwork on the right, may be seen the end of the first cellar; before the erection of this brickwork it would have been possible to walk a complete square of passageways. Also at the end, but on the left, a steep bank of sand leads up to what was another exit 13 feet away, now blocked up, which would have emerged at the upper end of Victoria Terrace. Looking back down this passage, two more good examples of bands of ironstone can be seen extending up one wall and across the roof to the opposite wall.

Returning to the entrance to the second cellar observe again the flight of stairs. The steps descending to the right were already badly worn when the Local History Group starting showing visitors round in 1968, whereas the steps ascending to the left, although worn, were in nowhere as bad a state. This suggests that the original entrance, at the top of these stairs was, after a comparatively short period of time, abandoned in favour of the South Street entrance; it did reduce the number of steps to be climbed by 13! That original entrance would be under the Victorian buildings and formerly under or in the grounds of one of the old cottages which were situated on the hill prior to Victoria Terrace being built.

On descending the stairs, apart from noticing the original worn steps to the left of the hand rail, the other feature is the height of the roof, which to begin with is just over head high but progresses to being 11 feet above the ground at the end of the first flight. At the turn of the stairs on the left hand wall are the initials, JS, EC, and WC, and cut in to the wall on the right are the indents presumed to have been made by ropes hauling up sacks of sand. The initials PG are on the left hand wall as the descent of the second flight is commenced, and after a few steps on the right is the inscription PCH 1889. Continuing down on the right are what appears to be ASWTSK 1875 and RWT. At this point the main well is seen again to the right, a brick-arch built into the shaft affording a small 'landing' from which it is possible to look up to the higher brick-arch which was the means of crossing the well from the wine cellar. Half-way up to that point in the shaft can be seen the oldest clear date discovered so far, that of 1672, together with the letters TLWCWCE, presumably a combination of initials.

On the landing itself, facing towards the well are several inscriptions. To the right:- WSH., FXP., MR 1875, RFC, T.WRIGHT 1873, WR1875 and, alongside the initials RCG, a date which resembles 1666 but is

probably 1866. On the left:- C. Letts, R. Perring 1873, FW, EW, H.H. Young 1882 (H. Harman Young was the last owner of the Caves; the Young family were brewers and maltsters in the town for many years), JT 1863, CG 1825, WWT 1823, I. HOARE 1765 and W. HOARE 1765 (who died in his 50s in 1776 according to his gravestone in St. Martin's Churchyard).

Turning back to the stairs, on the facing wall are numerous more inscriptions, in descending order:- RP 1873, GJ 1873, ER, WAR 1855, FWK 1785, PGA, HAK, JW 1825 JHK 1825, A Peacock 1796, RG, KP, JHK 1871, EW 1753, 1750, EH 1824, P. Cook (a Philip Cook died in 1832 according to a gravestone in the churchyard), WC 1752, MPS 1871, MS 1749, RL 1871, and RP again.

On the right hand side of the stairs, also in descending order, are:- WH 1760, EM, Palmer, WSS 1890, CMP, JM 1845, F. PULLAN, HY 1866, IK 1834, HS 1838, WR and HS 1873.

At this point the stairs take a final turn 90 degree turn to the right, there being three more original steps. On the facing wall before the foot of these steps are the following:- CGK, WP, LP 1885, GDW 1753, FHC 1743, IC, WB 1763, GL 1865, HY 1746, CL 1855. (The old style of writing the letter 'W' until the early part of the 19th century was virtually a 'double V' rather than a 'double U').

Here then is the lowest point in the caves complex with the cavern (the dimensions of which are eight and a half feet across, nine and a half feet wide and just over six feet high) at four feet from the foot of the stairs; on the right can be seen the bottom of the well shaft (75 feet beneath the surface). The black stain caused by the water remaining at a constant level for many years can be clearly seen at the base of the shaft, reaching to a height of 57 inches, and also in the cavern up to two inches above the carved-out ledge or seat. The opening into the well from the passage appears to have been hewn as an afterthought or could it even have been by mistake? Once the hole was made the spring water at that level would have surged into the cavern flooding it to that same depth and it seems inconceivable anyone would wish to remain seated in that chamber partially immersed in cold water. It is said the spring was 'crystalline and pure' but it was also icy cold. One supposition is that it was deliberately done to adapt the cavern's original purpose to being a place of baptism, again possibly by those of puritan beliefs. Unfortunately this is just one more mystery of these caves, the answers to which we can only guess. More inscriptions appear in the chamber:- WSH 1812, HR 1815, RCG 1866, PP, EP, JR 1873, RFG, AND T. WRIGHT 1873.

Here the tour ends; a climb up the 40 steps leads back to the entrance, and into daylight but also into the hustle and bustle of the 'outside world' again, leaving behind the cool tranquility, and a few enigmas, of a bygone era.

xxxxxxxxxxxxxxxx

## REFERENCES

Anon. "Smugglers' Caves as Wine Cellars." Article in "The Wine and Spirit Trade Record." 1924.

Aubrey, J. "The Natural History and Antiquities of the County of Surrey." 1719.

Bastian, F. "Daniel Defoe and the Dorking District." Surrey Archaeological Collections. Vol.55. 1957.

Bright, J.S. "A history of Dorking." 1884.

Dennis, J. "Handbook of Dorking." 2nd ed. 1858.

Malden, H.E. "Rose Hill House and its Neighbourhood in Dorking." 1930.

Timbs, J. "A picturesque promenade round Dorking." 2nd ed. 1823.

Tyson, D.E. "A Dorking Childhood - Memories of Old Dorking." Ed. M.L. Felgate. 1979.